W9-BXX-934

One of the best feelings
in the whole world
comes from being a friend...
and having a friend in return.

— Lorrie Westfall

Blue Mountain Arts®
Bestselling Titles

By Susan Polis Schutz:
To My Daughter, with Love, on the Important Things in Life
To My Son, with Love
I Love You

By Douglas Pagels:
100 Things to Always Remember... and One Thing to Never Forget
For You, Just Because You're Very Special to Me
To the One Person I Consider to Be My Soul Mate

Is It Time to Make a Change?
by Deanna Beisser

To the Love of My Life
by Donna Fargo

A Lifetime of Love ...Poems on the Passages of Life
by Leonard Nimoy

Anthologies:
Always Believe in Yourself and Your Dreams
For You, My Daughter
I Love You, Mom
I'm Glad You Are My Sister
Marriage Is a Promise of Love
May You Always Have an Angel by Your Side
Take Each Day One Step at a Time
Teaching and Learning Are Lifelong Journeys
There Is Greatness Within You, My Son
Think Positive Thoughts Every Day
To My Child
With God by Your Side ...You Never Have to Be Alone

Good Friends
Come Along Once
in a Lifetime

A Blue Mountain Arts® Collection
on All the Wonderful Things
Friendship Brings to Life

Edited by Gary Morris

Blue Mountain Press™
Boulder, Colorado

Copyright © 2004 by Blue Mountain Arts, Inc.

All rights reserved. No part of this publication may be reproduced, stored in a retrieval system or transmitted in any form or by any means, electronic, mechanical, photocopying, recording or otherwise, without the written permission of the publisher.

We wish to thank Susan Polis Schutz for permission to reprint the following poems that appear in this publication: "Our Friendship Will Remain Constant" and "You Are Always My Friend." Copyright © 1982, 1985 by Stephen Schutz and Susan Polis Schutz. All rights reserved.

Library of Congress Control Number: 2003114535
ISBN: 0-88396-797-9

ACKNOWLEDGMENTS appear on page 64.

Certain trademarks are used under license.
BLUE MOUNTAIN PRESS is registered in U.S. Patent and Trademark Office.

Printed in China.
First Printing: 2004

♲ This book is printed on recycled paper.
This book is printed on fine quality, laid embossed, 80 lb. paper. This paper has been specially produced to be acid free (neutral pH) and contains no groundwood or unbleached pulp. It conforms with all the requirements of the American National Standards Institute, Inc., so as to ensure that this book will last and be enjoyed by future generations.

Blue Mountain Arts, Inc.
P.O. Box 4549, Boulder, Colorado 80306

Contents

Rare People

There are rare people in this world
who are so caring —
   whose natural instinct is to put
   someone else's needs
   ahead of their own;
who offer encouragement
   when it is needed;
who are always there to listen
   with a smile and a loving,
   open heart.

There are rare people
   who never want or expect
      praise for their good deeds
      because that's just
         the way they are.

   You are one of
   those rare people...

How fortunate I am
that you are my friend!

— Andrea L. Hines

Friends like You
Come Along
Once in a Lifetime...

And I want you to know how glad I am that you came along in mine. Friends like you are so valuable and so rare. You provide me with things that can't compare with any other happiness in my life. I am so thankful for all the wonderful things about you. You understand my difficulties and always give me the benefit of the doubt. There are so many times when you're the only one who knows what I'm going through. You're what communication and trust are all about.

If you sense that I'm hurting, you do whatever you can to help me. And you don't hold things against me. You help me prop up my courage if it starts to fade, and you have such a gentle way of providing reassurance.

You walk beside me when I could use a little guidance and direction in my life. And, more than anyone else, you support me in my attempts to do what is right.

You multiply my smiles and you constantly add to my favorite memories. You make me feel like I really am somebody who matters. Then you quietly prove to me how beautiful that feeling is. You really are amazing. And I wish I had a way to thank you for all this.

I feel like it's important to let you know that, in you, I have come across a wonderful, once-in-a-lifetime friend. The gift of that friendship is the nicest thing anyone could ever give... and I will cherish it all the days of my life and all the years that I live.

— Emilia Larson

"Thank You"
Just Doesn't Seem
like Enough

Two words. Eight letters.

"Thank you" just doesn't seem like
   enough to express my gratitude
   for all you've done.

It doesn't seem like enough to say,
   "What would I do without you?"
   It doesn't seem like enough of an
   exchange for all you've given me.

But that's the most amazing part...
   you give of yourself, expecting
   nothing in return.

I wish there were words to express
   how much I appreciate all you've
   done — how much I appreciate you.

But there are no words, except two
   small ones that come directly from
   my heart... thank you!

— Donna Gephart

My Definition of a Good Friend Is You

Good friends aren't picky and delicate, and their friendship is not easily broken. They don't have to be handled with kid gloves or tiptoed around. They are tough and trusting and loyal to each other. They want the best for each other. They do things for each other. They are easy and comfortable to be with. When they're not around, we miss them and our world seems out of balance. They are the kind of friends who stand by each other no matter what. When they say they mean forever, they really do.

Good friends have no need to question each other's motives. They know that they're on each other's side, not in competition with each other, and they would never do the other any harm. They wouldn't hurt each other's feelings for anything and they would go to great lengths to protect their friendship because they know it's so special.

There are many ways to define a good friend, but I will cut it short by just saying that... my definition of a good friend is you.

— Donna Fargo

The First Time I Met You, I Knew We Would Be Friends

We connected immediately with mutual interests and easy, natural conversations. When we're together, I feel relaxed and comfortable. I am more myself with you than I am with anyone else I know.

I love how we laugh and have fun together. We never run out of things to talk about. I confide in you with complete faith and trust. Your friendship has brought a new sense of peace and equanimity into my life. It has allowed me to examine my own life and graciously taught me how to be gentler with the person I am.

Your friendship has brought me a newfound sense of confidence and self-worth. It has given me a special love that remains loyal and true. As a friend, you've given me a piece of your heart. I am fortunate to be blessed with the wonderful experiences we've had. I am deeply honored to have you as my friend.

— Debbie Burton-Peddle

As the Years Pass By...

It is easier to see
who the special people are in my life.
It's easier to realize what is important,
what matters, who matters.
Please know, my friend,
that you are very important
and you matter so very much to me.
As I journey along the path of my life,
sharing some steps
along the way with you,
I am touched by your kindness,
I am warmed by your caring,
and I am blessed by your friendship.

Today and every day,
you deserve to be touched
with the treasures of life's precious gifts;
you deserve to be blessed
with the goodness of friends,
the generosity of love,
and graces from God.
May all your days be as special
as you are.

— Denise Johnston

I Celebrate Our Friendship Every Day

You are the type of friend that
people search endlessly for —
a person so caring and kind
so honest and understanding

You are a person who finds the right words
and whose silence is so comforting
when there are none
You are the one person
who has never let me down
the one I run to first when something
exciting happens in my day
the one who carries the umbrella
when life's storm clouds blow in

You have made such a difference
every day of my life
making the tough decisions
a little bit easier
and the wonderful times
so much more memorable

Together we've laughed harder
and talked about our dreams
We've pushed each other to strive
for the very best
and padded each fall
with reassurance and understanding

In our lives we will share many gifts
with many people
but I want you to know
that our friendship is a gift
I am thankful for every day of my life

— Elle Mastro

You've Planted
Some Beautiful Seeds
in the Garden of My Life

In the garden of life,
seed-planters are people
who cultivate and nurture others.
Seed-planters sow seeds
   of faith and encouragement
and they always believe
   the best in you.

You have been a seed-planter
   in my life.
With your tender care,
   I have blossomed —
and my heart is forever thankful
   for you.

— Autumn Banks

I Keep Our Memories Tucked Within My Heart

Inside my heart
there is this little place
It keeps me warm
It keeps me sane
It is my sunshine on
    rainy days

This is the place where
I've stored away
each memory we have shared
and all the wonderful thoughts
    I think of you

So no matter where you are
or how far away I go
I will keep you close to me
and my heart will be filled
    with happiness always

— Deana Marino

Thanks for Giving Me the Gift of True Friendship

True friendship is that unexplained heart connection between two people who enrich each other's life. They may not know exactly why they became friends, but they do know that their presence in each other's life is a gift...

True friendship is one of the most valuable treasures anyone could have. It is necessary nourishment to the heart and soul. It creates a feeling of unconditional acceptance between two people who allow each other to be themselves — just as they are.

True friends are sensitive to each other's
own perceived flaws, insecurities, vanities,
peculiarities, and opinions, but neither
puts demands on the other to change.
They just want the best for each other...
always. This kind of relationship takes
no effort and needs no rules.

This is our kind of friendship... the
kind that exists between two people who
understand each other and know how to
communicate with each other — often
by not saying a word.

Thanks for giving me the gift of
true friendship.

— Donna Fargo

You and I Are Bigger than Any of Our Differences

We are different people,
   you and I.
We have different interests,
   opinions, ideas,
and ways of doing things.
Sometimes, these differences
lead to friction between us.
Those times can be frustrating,
   uncomfortable, and discouraging...
but they don't detract from
the important place you have in my life.
You have so many qualities
   I admire and appreciate.
I value your insight and advice;
I respect your knowledge and wisdom.
So though our differences may seem
   to push us apart...
always remember there is
   so much more
      that pulls us together.

— Carrie Cramer

Our Friendship Will Remain Constant

Sometimes we do not feel like we want to feel
Sometimes we do not achieve what we want
    to achieve
Sometimes things that happen do not make sense
Sometimes life leads us in directions that are
beyond our control
It is at these times, most of all
that we need someone
who will quietly understand us
and be there to support us
I want you to know, my friend
that I am here for you
in every way
and remember that though
circumstances in our lives change
our friendship will always remain constant
and remember that though
things may be difficult now
tomorrow is a new day

— Susan Polis Schutz

Old Friends Are the Best

Old friendship is companionship
   turned golden;
it takes on a luster like ivory
where love's light has lingered.
Old friends are threads of gold
   in the tapestry of our lives.
They hold things together,
   keep us connected,
and help our world make sense.
Old friends know where we've been,
   where we are,
and where we want to go.
They encourage us to dream,
   and if those dreams fall apart
they're the ones who stay
   and help us pick up the pieces.
They help us build our lives
   better and stronger.

With their unconditional caring,
  they give us the courage
to endure the hard times.
They show us what is best
  and beautiful in ourselves,
and they are gentle and quiet
  with our faults.
An old friend is a kindred spirit,
  confidant, and companion
    in life's journey;
the one person we utterly trust,
  who knows us totally as we are.
When all else has come and gone
  in our lives,
old friends remain.
They are friends for life —
  like you and me.

— Vickie M. Worsham

The Friendship Wish

With the rising of the sun each morning, I wish you beauty and a day filled with wonder and promise. At night, as the sun slides peacefully into her cradle, I wish you contentment and the knowledge that you have lived the day, not simply survived it. And in between, I wish you all this...

A heart filled with joy by small and wondrous things — the sweet song of a bird; the ringing, gleeful sound of a child's laughter; or even just a memory that puts a smile in your step.

A life filled with passion. Indulge in lingering kisses and spontaneous hugs. Use strong language; get angry at injustice. Raise your voice, snort with laughter; don't be afraid to be seen or heard, for you are worth noticing.

The courage to face all that life has to offer:
the good, the bad, and the boring in-between.
Imagine beyond your limits, whatever they
may be, and never be stifled by ignorance.

The wisdom to heed the beat of your own
heart. This is your dance — you set the
tempo. Why line dance when you can rumba?

Mostly, though, I wish you love. Contrary to
what some people might say or think, I believe
it is okay to go around loving everything —
trees, cats, flowers, cars, birds, songs, hats,
husbands, kids, furniture, parents, clouds,
rainbows, brothers, sisters, fish, sitcoms,
paintings, jellybeans, flannel pajamas,
chocolate, coffee, cinnamon tea — because
all these things make up the life you live.

Let yourself love whatever you wish, my friend,
and all my wishes for you will come true.

— Kathy Larson

Friendship Is...

...creating a sunny day together, even if it is pouring rain outside.

...making time for each other no matter how busy life gets.

...standing up for one another when challenges and confrontations come along.

...dropping everything when the other person is in need.

...loving each other unconditionally.

...dreaming, planning, and believing together.

...laughing until you can hardly breathe — and not caring who hears you.

...sharing cherished memories and priceless moments that will last for a lifetime.

— Jane Andrews

We Go Together Like...

Cookies and milk
candles and birthday cake
ghost stories and campfires

We go together like...
pillow fights and laughter
blush and mascara
sleepovers and truth-or-dare

We go together like...
music and dancing
pictures and frames
popcorn and movies

We go together like...
winter and snow
spring and cherry blossoms
stars and the night

We go together like...
best friends

— Dallas Woodburn

You're My All-Time Greatest Friend

When I was five, my best friend was the person I played with until near-sunset. Only one of our mother's voices telling us to come inside meant that playtime was over for the day.

At seven, I just knew that my best friend was the person who sat next to me in school — the one I gave the first piece of cake to at my birthday party.

As a teenager, "best friend" meant something different. The person who listened to me and still liked me afterward fit the definition best.

I met you when I was grown up, and our friendship has taught me that being best friends means all this... and so much more.

True enough, we play together... at this game called life. If I had a birthday party, you'd definitely get the first piece of cake. You are undoubtedly the person who listens to me and still likes me when I'm done pouring out all the stuff that makes for trials and triumphs in life.

Through the years, though, our friendship has transcended the issue of birthday cakes, and some of our heart-to-heart conversations have subsided into silence. It's so often not about words; we can sit in complete silence and get up knowing that we've had the best conversation ever.

That kind of friendship doesn't come overnight, and I just want to thank you for being my best friend at a time when life makes it so necessary to have one.

You know what? I have this feeling that even if life didn't make it necessary, we'd still be best friends. We really don't need any reason at all. Thank you.

— Patrice A. Francis

"That's just what good friends do"

Just like everyone else, I have times when I know that I can't do it all by myself. There are times when I need encouragement and some extra strength, a bit of wisdom, a little humor, and a lot of knowing that someone is on my side. It may be a situation that needs some gentle understanding; it might be a problem that needs to be talked out. There are so many aspects of my life that benefit tremendously by a friend — just "listening in" and then sharing insights that could only come from someone on the inside. There are times when the only thing that sees me through... is the friend I have in you.

I do have you for a friend. And that is so wonderful. I want you to be my friend. That is forever. And yes, I gladly and graciously admit that... I need you to be my friend.

I tell you that truthfully, honestly, and openly. I want you to receive it as the compliment it's meant to be. It says in a roundabout way that you are the one person I know I can turn to. And whether I'm dealing with a crisis or just cruising along, it makes all the difference in the world to know that a smile is in your eyes when you see me... and that there is someone I can share everything with.

Why am I telling you all this? It's because I want to say that everything I have with you... you have with me.

You can call on me, turn to me, and count on me to be there for you wherever, whenever. Because you so generously share the laughter, I will lovingly dry any tears. Because you so kindly believe in me, I will never stop believing in you. I will cheer you on and do whatever I can to help you reach out for your hopes and dreams. But I'll also be there to protect you, to ease any burdens, and to remind you that there are two of us to overpower any worries and chase away any fears.

I am your friend. You can rely on me, you can depend on me, and yes, I would be honored if you would need me, too. When two people are as close as we are, the giving and the taking blend together into one. There's no keeping score. There's just giving more.

That's just what good friends do.

— Douglas Pagels

I'm Glad
I Know You, Friend

Every once in a while,
I stop and wonder
what my life would be like
if you and I had never
crossed paths...

You are so much
a part of me —
my life,
my thoughts,
and my heart —
that it's impossible to imagine
what my life would be like
if you weren't in it.

I am certain of
at least one thing, though...

I wouldn't smile as much,
laugh as much,
or love as much
without you here.

— Rachyl Taylor

We Share the Things That Really Matter

Great big smiles,
out-of-control laughter,
and much-needed hugs
are some of the most precious
    things to me.
There's no one who brings
more of these to my life than you...

The time we share together —
having a heartfelt conversation
or simply being in
    each other's presence —
could never be replaced
    by material things.
That's because our friendship
has a value that can't be measured.

I'm so happy that you're my friend.
You bring the best things in life
right to my doorstep.

— Jane Andrews

A Place in My Heart

Quietly, without pretense,
with total honesty and care,
you wandered into my heart
and found a special place.

This place in my heart
is now yours alone.
It is full of warmth and care,
love and strength.
It's a place called friendship.
You touched things in me
that were long forgotten,
and brought back to life
the joy of laughter
and the comfort of being myself.

In return, please know
that when you need somewhere to hide
or share your dreams,
you'll find that place in me.

Don't be afraid to stumble
or need the comfort of a hand
to help you through the night —
you'll find that strength in me.
When you need time to be
the person few others see
or the comfort of a friend
to listen to your fears —
you'll find that friend in me.

Please know that I am here
to share your joy, laughter,
    and pain.
I am here to be whatever you need
    to help you through your life.
I will never be too far away —
because you are a friend forever
    in my heart.

— Larry L. Black

As a Friend, You've Made a Difference in My Life

Sometimes it's easy to think that because we're not famous, maybe we're not important.

I want you to know that you don't need to be a movie star, a bestselling author, an inventor, a millionaire, or anything other than the special person you are to be a hero to me.

I hope you know how much you mean to me and what an important part you play in my life. When I look back through the years, it's easy to see that you've always been there to support me and to tell me that I could accomplish anything I could imagine.

You've laughed with me, cried with me, and dreamed my dreams with me.

I just wanted to take this moment to tell you that all you are and all you've done for me have not gone unnoticed.

I don't know how I would have made it through the hard times without you to lean on...
and the good times could never have been as good without you to share them with me.

If you ever wonder whether you've made a contribution in this life, know that you've made a beautiful, wonderful difference in my world.

— Jason Blume

A Friendship Flower

You would think
that we might have
forgotten each other
by now; life is so
uncertain — so many
people come and go,
like rain. But no
matter where I have
stood, or what
roads I've been
down, you have
been there for
me — at every turn
along the way...

...and I guess
that some things
change and other
things don't
and there are
some special
types of
friendships that
grow and yet stay
the same. And
I'm just really
glad we've got
that special sort
of friendship... that
is there for you,
there for you
always.
Thanks for being a friend.

— Ashley Rice

You're Appreciated
for Everything
You Are

I have the sweet and special privilege of being your friend. And I know how wonderful you are... in every facet of your life. One of the most beautiful aspects of all is knowing what an incredible person you are.

You always go out of your way to do so many things for others. You never hesitate to take time out of your life to make other lives shine brighter.

You have a heart of pure gold, and you just
seem to know what is needed and how best
to help. It is so natural for you to share the
treasure of all that you are,
so unselfishly...

You do the things you do in
the most admirable way of all...
from a heart that loves so much
and that only wants what's
best for everyone.

And I know that you could hear
it every day and still never get
to hear — nearly often enough —
all the thanks you deserve.

I'd like to be among those who hope you
will remember your whole life through
that you are appreciated so much
for all that you are
and for everything
that you do.

— R. L. Keith

Thanks for Being So Special

Every once in a while
you meet a special person
who helps you through
the rough spots
and makes you laugh
and understands the words
you make up
when you are stressed
or running at a million miles
    an hour.

Every once in a while,
you meet a special friend
like that...
who makes you remember
things like crayons and rainbows
and good days...
And suddenly everything
seems possible again.

Thanks for being that friend.

— Ashley Rice

Friends like You Make the World a Better Place

Friends are the joys
that make us more like family
and the moments that show us
we still live in a caring world.

Friends are the added strength we need
to face what life may bring;
they are always close at hand,
bringing hope to the soul.
They have arms full of caring;
they are there to soften every hurt.
They are thoughts and feelings shared
    but never labeled.
Friends are candles lit by one another;
they are the glow of time and memory
to warm our hearts.

— Linda E. Knight

A Best Friend...
Is What You'll
Always Be to Me

A best friend...
one who walks the extra mile with you —
    a smile-maker, hope-giver,
        heart-warmer, and hand-holder.

A best friend...
one who concentrates on your
    emotional well-being
by bringing to light past victories,
keeping you focused on the positive,
and reminding you that you're not alone;
one who will not rest until
    you see life's brighter side.

A best friend...
one who reminds you it's just a few
    more steps to the finish line
        and you can't stop now.

A best friend...
one who cares so much that it shows
each time you need
    a voice of inspiration,
        an arm around your shoulder,
    and the presence of someone
        who cares completely about you.

A best friend...
that's what you are to me
and what I'll always be to you.

— Barbara J. Hall

I Wish I Could Explain How Much You Mean to Me

There have been so many times when I've wanted to find a way to tell you just how much you mean to me. I've looked for cards that say just the right words, gifts that express just the right sentiment, hugs that wrap up all my feelings and put them straight into your heart. But in the end, I always feel as if I've missed something.

Sometimes I think there must be nothing in this world that is strong enough to explain how much I care for you. Maybe there's nothing I could ever say or do or give you that would make you understand just how wonderful I think you are and how glad I am to have you in my life...

But that doesn't mean I'm ever going to stop trying.

— Carol Thomas

You Are Always My Friend

You are always my friend
when I am happy
or when I am sad
when I am all alone
or when I am with people
You are always my friend
if I see you today
or if I see you
   a year from now
if I talk to you today
or if I talk to you
   a year from now
You are always my friend
and though through the years
we will change
it doesn't matter what I do
or it doesn't matter what you do
Throughout our lifetime
you are always my friend

— Susan Polis Schutz

If There Were One Thing I Could Give You...

If there were one thing I could give you, it would be the power to make your life everything you've always dreamed it could be.

I would give you the strength to look past the everyday concerns of life and reach out for all the dreams in your heart.

I would give you the wings you need to soar... and the courage to jump.

I would give you the motivation to keep seeking out the best in life, and the patience to keep trying until it is yours.

I would give you the inspiration to listen to whatever your heart whispers, and the confidence to follow wherever it leads.

I would give you the faith to make wishes on falling stars and know that they will all come true.

Most of all, I would give you the power to realize that all these things are already yours... if you only believe in yourself the way I believe in you.

— Rachyl Taylor

I Can Never
Repay You, My Friend...

I tried to think of something
I could give you
that would signify all you mean to me.
It had to be something very special
because that's what you are.
It had to be something that would last,
just as our friendship has
   all these years.
So I took all my memories of us
and added the laughter,
the secrets, and the comforting and
   encouraging words we've shared,
then stirred them all together.
I sprinkled it with faith,
   mixed in a promise of forever,
      and sealed it with love.
Because all along I knew
   that there is no greater gift
than the wonderful friendship we share,
and all I can ever hope to do
   is give it back to you.

— Barbara Cage

You Are a Gift
to the World

Your friendship is priceless,
your caring is my treasure,
and your smile is all it takes
to brighten each day.
Your kindness is my comfort,
your friendship is a wonderful gift,
and your laughter is light
for each day's journey.
Knowing someone like you
is like having a rainbow on my doorstep
every season of the year.
You add color to the dullest days
and beauty to my dreams;
you help me search for all
    the treasures I hope to find.
Today, may your heart smile
knowing how much you are loved.
May every day bring you
all the wonderful discoveries
    you deserve,
just to remind you
what a wonderful gift you are
    to the world.

— Linda E. Knight

Friends Are
the Heartstrings of Life

Friends are such an important part
of life, and whether we see them
all the time or not, they are crucial
in the way we see and interact with
     the world.
Friends remind us that the sun is shining,
even though it might be hidden
behind some very threatening,
     dark clouds.
Friends stand by us and are there
to help through challenges,
illnesses, heartaches, and
all sorts of worries and decisions.
Friends keep us from losing our minds,
our faith, and sometimes
our spouses or our keys.

Friends play different roles, but
each one is important.
Some are the shoppers,
others the phone talkers,
some know just what to say
    when there's a tragedy,
and others make us laugh.
The one thing they all have in common
is that they bring camaraderie,
contentment, security, and joy
into our lives.

I'm so glad we're friends.
I feel very lucky to be part of your life...
and especially grateful
    that you are part of mine.

— Barbara Cage

Our Friendship
Is a Promise

Although we may not say it to each
other or even realize it, our friendship
is a promise.

It's a promise to always be there for the
other person — no matter what.

It's a promise to share bits and pieces of
our lives with each other.

It's a promise to care so much about the
other person that one's laughter belongs
to the other, as do one's tears.

It's a promise that no distance will ever
put space between two hearts... the
hearts of true friends.

Yes, our friendship is a promise — a
promise of support and laughter and
hope. A promise of loyalty and love
and caring that will grow stronger
with each day.

Our friendship is a promise... that will
last a lifetime.

— Donna Gephart

We'll Always Be There for Each Other

There is no greater feeling
Than knowing that someone
Is truly there for you.

It is a comfort beyond measure
To know that you can trust
Your life and your heart
To someone who forever understands.
To have someone who always
Makes you feel better with just
The right words
Offers solace beyond compare.

To be uplifted in such an effortless way
That you almost come to expect it
Is a rarity to be treasured.

For this I give
My heartfelt thanks
And my love to you,
Dear Friend,
Now and always.
Thank you for the joy
That you bring to
My world every day.

— Lynn Barnhart

To a Friend Who Is like an Angel to Me

In this life, on this earth, and in the days that I spend trying to do the best I can, I know that I wouldn't be half the person I am if it weren't for a little divine inspiration that comes from having a friend like you.

You have been my saving grace on more occasions than you will ever know. You are my friend, my see-me-through and inspire-my-smile companion. When you listen, you hear what I'm really trying to say. And when you communicate, your words come straight from the heart.

You make me feel that "yes, my presence really does matter!" You constantly add to my joys and to the value of my self-worth, and I wish I could thank you every day.

You are so amazing. Compared to you, I feel like I'll always be in training for my own set of wings. You are my very own down-to-earth angel. I cherish you very much, and I want to thank you, my dear friend, for the way you bring so much joy to my life.

— Marin McKay

I'm so lucky to have a friend like you

One of the best feelings
in the whole world
comes from being a friend...
and having a friend in return.

I wouldn't trade my friendship with
you for anything... because I know that
nothing else could ever begin to bring me
the contentment, the wonderful
craziness, the support and the caring,
the laughter, the understanding, and
all the thousands of things that we
share together...

One of the sweetest feelings
in the whole world
comes from knowing that
everything we share — and the joy
that graces our lives — will warm our
hearts forever, in all the days ahead.

For no matter how far apart
our paths may wander,
and no matter how long it's been,
it's so great to know that...

you and I will always be
the closest and
dearest of friends.

— Lorrie Westfall

May You Always Know How Much I Care

A long time ago we built something between us that is still so strong, so special, and so lasting. I feel connected to you in ways that are hard to explain, yet they are filled with meaning and they speak to my soul.

I am so glad life brought you my way — directing your path into my life and giving me a friend to share with and care about.

Today, stop for a moment and let the memories we have made hold your heart — and please know how very much I care. You are very important to me, and you always will be.

I want you to know that no matter where your life takes you, you will always have a place in my heart.

— Denise Johnston

ACKNOWLEDGMENTS

We gratefully acknowledge the permission granted by the following authors and authors' representatives to reprint poems or excerpts from their publications.

PrimaDonna Entertainment Corp. for "My Definition of a Good Friend Is You" and "Thanks for Giving Me the Gift of True Friendship" by Donna Fargo. Copyright © 2002, 2003 by PrimaDonna Entertainment Corp. All rights reserved.

Debbie Burton-Peddle for "The First Time I Met You, I Knew We Would Be Friends." Copyright © 2004 by Debbie Burton-Peddle. All rights reserved.

Autumn Banks for "You've Planted Some Beautiful Seeds in the Garden of My Life." Copyright © 2004 by Autumn Banks. All rights reserved.

Carrie Cramer for "You and I Are Bigger than Any of Our Differences." Copyright © 2004 by Carrie Cramer. All rights reserved.

Vickie M. Worsham for "Old Friends Are the Best." Copyright © 2004 by Vickie M. Worsham. All rights reserved.

Kathy Larson for "The Friendship Wish." Copyright © 2004 by Kathy Larson. All rights reserved.

Dallas Woodburn for "We Go Together Like...." Copyright © 2004 by Dallas Woodburn. All rights reserved.

Patrice A. Francis for "You're My All-Time Greatest Friend." Copyright © 2004 by Patrice A. Francis. All rights reserved.

Larry L. Black for "A Place in My Heart." Copyright © 2004 by Larry L. Black. All rights reserved.

Jason Blume for "As a Friend, You've Made a Difference in My Life." Copyright © 2004 by Jason Blume. All rights reserved.

Barbara J. Hall for "A Best Friend... Is What You'll Always Be to Me." Copyright © 2004 by Barbara J. Hall. All rights reserved.

Barbara Cage for "Friends Are the Heartstrings of Life." Copyright © 2004 by Barbara Cage. All rights reserved.

Donna Gephart for "Our Friendship Is a Promise." Copyright © 2004 by Donna Gephart. All rights reserved.

A careful effort has been made to trace the ownership of selections used in this anthology in order to obtain permission to reprint copyrighted material and give proper credit to the copyright owners. If any error or omission has occurred, it is completely inadvertent, and we would like to make corrections in future editions provided that written notification is made to the publisher:

BLUE MOUNTAIN ARTS, INC., P.O. Box 4549, Boulder, Colorado 80306.